学校 - school	2
旅行 - travel	5
交通运输 - transport	8
城市 - city	10
地形 - landscape	14
餐馆 - restaurant	17
超市 - supermarket	20
饮料 - drinks	22
食物 - food	23
农场 - farm	27
房子 - house	31
客厅 - living room	33
厨房 - kitchen	35
浴室 - bathroom	38
儿童房 - child's room	42
衣服 - clothing	44
办公室 - office	49
经济 - economy	51
职业 - occupations	53
工具 - tools	56
乐器 - musical instruments	57
动物园 - zoo	59
体育 - sports	62
活动 - activities	63
家 - family	67
身体 - body	68
医院 - hospital	72
紧急情况 - emergency	76
地球 - earth	77
钟表 - clock	79
周 - week	80
年 - year	81
形状 - shapes	83
颜色 - colors	84
反义词 - opposites	85
数字 - numbers	88
语言 - languages	90
谁/什么/怎样 - who / what / how	91
方位 - where	92

Impressum
Verlag: BABADADA GmbH, Nedderfeld 112 , 22529 Hamburg
Geschäftsführer / Verlagsleitung: Harald Hof
Druck: Books on Demand GmbH, In de Tarpen 42, 22848 Norderstedt

Imprint
Publisher: BABADADA GmbH, Nedderfeld 112 , 22529 Hamburg, Germany
Managing Director / Publishing direction: Harald Hof
Print: Books on Demand GmbH, In de Tarpen 42, 22848 Norderstedt, Germany

学校
school

除 divide
黑板 board
教室 classroom
校园 school yard
老师 teacher
纸 paper
钢笔 pen
办公桌 desk
书写 write
直尺 ruler
书 book
学生 pupil

书包
satchel

铅笔盒
pencil case

铅笔
pencil

卷笔刀
pencil sharpener

橡皮擦
rubber

画板
drawing pad

图画
drawing

画笔
paintbrush

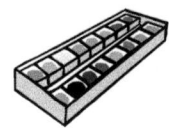
颜料盒
paint box

剪刀
scissors

胶水
glue

练习册
exercise book

家庭作业
homework

数字
number

加
add

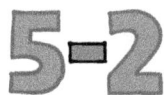
减
subtract

乘
multiply

计算
calculate

字母
letter

字母表
alphabet

字
word

学校 - school

课文
text

读
read

粉笔
chalk

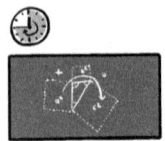
上课
lesson

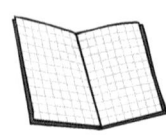
登记
register

考试
examination

证书
certificate

校服
school uniform

教育
education

百科全书
encyclopedia

大学
university

显微镜
microscope

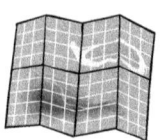
地图
map

废纸筐
waste-paper basket

旅行

travel

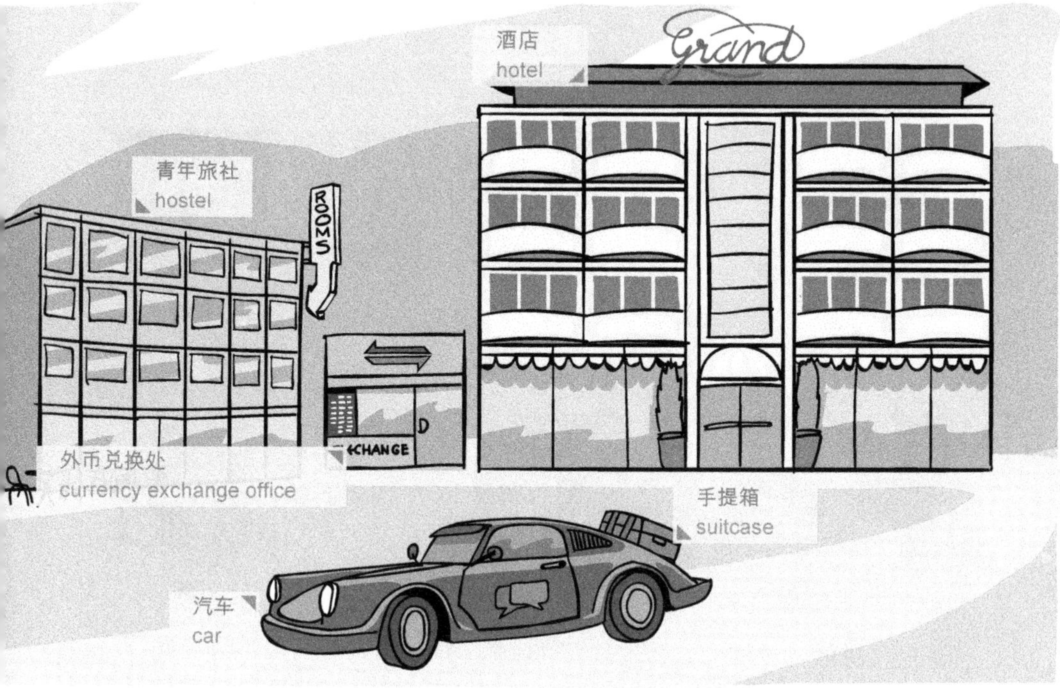
酒店
hotel
Grand
青年旅社
hostel
ROOMS
外币兑换处
currency exchange office
EXCHANGE
手提箱
suitcase
汽车
car

语言

language

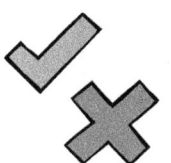

是/否

yes / no

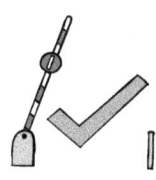

好的

Okay

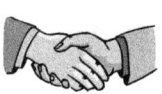

您好

hello

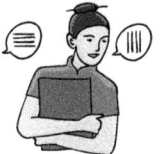

翻译员

translator

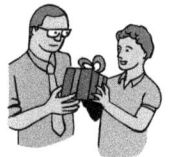

谢谢

Thank you

……多少钱？
how much is…?

我不明白
I do not understand

问题
problem

晚上好！
Good evening!

早上好！
Good morning!

晚安！
Good night!

再见
goodbye

方向
direction

行李
luggage

包
bag

双肩包
backpack

客人
guest

房间
room

睡袋
sleeping bag

帐篷
tent

旅游信息
tourist information

海滩
beach

信用卡
credit card

早餐
breakfast

午餐
lunch

晚餐
dinner

票
Ticket

电梯
elevator

邮票
stamp

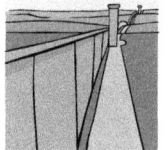

边界
border

海关
customs

大使馆
embassy

签证
visa

护照
passport

旅行 - travel

交通运输
transport

飞机 airplane

船 ship

消防车 fire truck

公交车 bus

卡车 truck

汽艇 motorboat

汽车 car

自行车 bike

摆渡船
ferry

小船
boat

摩托车
motorbike

警车
police car

赛车
racing car

租车
rental car

交通运输 - transport

拼车
car sharing

拖车
tow truck

垃圾车
garbage truck

发动机
engine

汽油
fuel

加油站
fuel station

交通标志
traffic sign

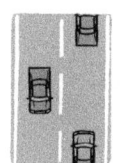
交通
traffic

交通堵塞
traffic jam

停车场
parking lot

火车站
train station

轨道
tracks

火车
train

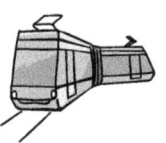
电车
tram

货车
wagon

交通运输 - transport

直升机
helicopter

机场
airport

塔
tower

乘客
passenger

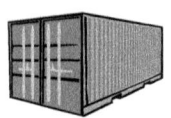
集装箱
container

纸板箱
carton

手推车
cart

篮子
basket

起飞/降落
take off / land

城市
city

村庄
village

市中心
city center

房子
house

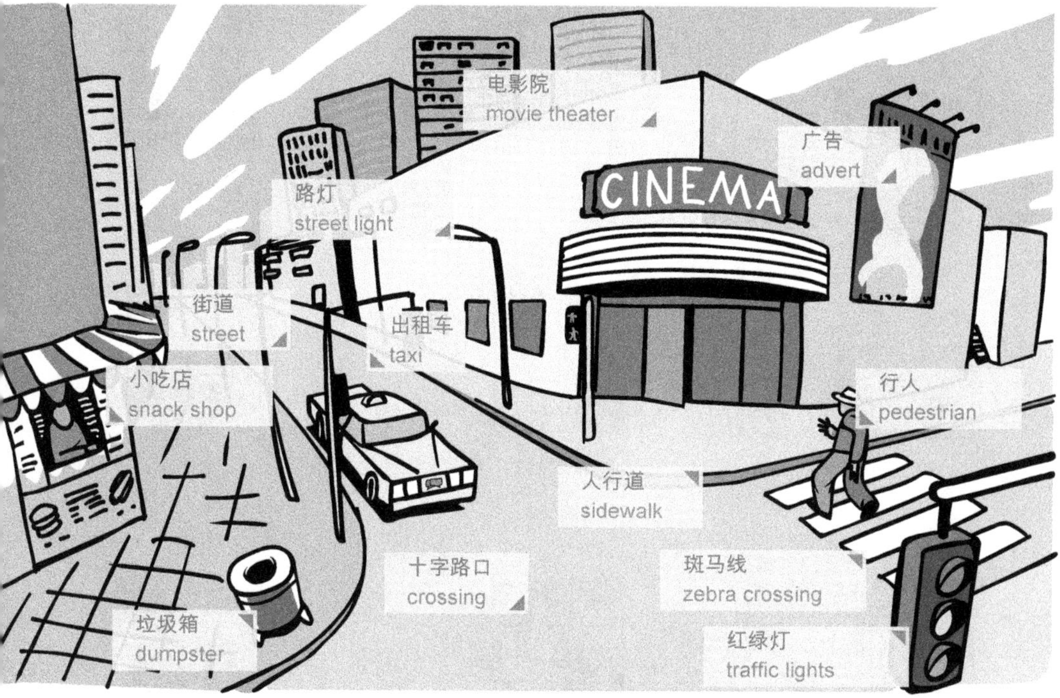
电影院
movie theater
广告
advert
CINEMA
路灯
street light
街道
street
出租车
taxi
小吃店
snack shop
行人
pedestrian
人行道
sidewalk
十字路口
crossing
斑马线
zebra crossing
垃圾箱
dumpster
红绿灯
traffic lights

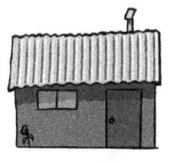

小屋

hut

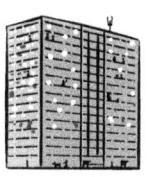

公寓

apartment

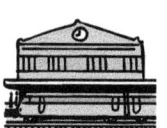

火车站

train station

市政厅

city hall

MUSEUM

博物馆

museum

学校

school

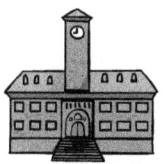

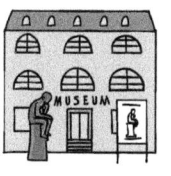

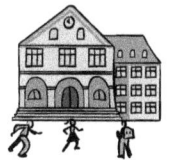

大学
university

银行
bank

医院
hospital

酒店
hotel

药房
pharmacy

办公室
office

书店
book shop

商店
shop

花店
flower shop

超市
supermarket

市场
market

百货商店
department store

鱼店
fishmonger's shop

购物中心
mall

海港
harbor

城市 - city

公园
park

长凳
bench

桥
bridge

楼梯
stairs

地铁
subway

隧道
tunnel

公交车站
bus stop

酒吧
bar

餐馆
restaurant

邮筒
postbox

路标
street sign

停车计时器
parking meter

动物园
zoo

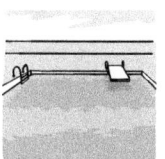
游泳馆
swimming pool

清真寺
mosque

城市 - city

农场
farm

污染
pollution

墓地
cemetery

教堂
church

操场
playground

寺庙
temple

地形
landscape

地形 - landscape

 峡谷 valley	 山 hill	 湖 lake
 森林 forest	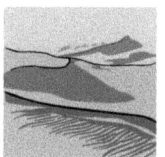 沙漠 desert	 火山 volcano
 城堡 castle	 彩虹 rainbow	 蘑菇 mushroom
 棕榈树 palm tree	 蚊子 mosquito	 苍蝇 fly
 蚂蚁 ant	 蜜蜂 bee	 蜘蛛 spider

地形 - landscape

 甲虫 beetle	 青蛙 frog	 松鼠 squirrel
 刺猬 hedgehog	 野兔 hare	 猫头鹰 owl
 鸟 bird	 天鹅 swan	 野猪 boar
 鹿 deer	 麋鹿 moose	 水坝 dam
 风力发电机 wind turbine	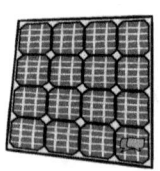 太阳能电池板 solar panel	 气候 climate

地形 - landscape

餐馆
restaurant

- 服务员 waiter
- 菜单 menu
- 椅子 chair
- 汤 soup
- 披萨饼 pizza
- 餐具 cutlery
- 桌布 tablecloth

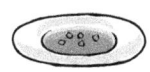

前菜 starter

主菜 main course

甜点 dessert

饮料 drinks

食物 food

瓶子 bottle

快餐
fast food

街边小吃
street food

茶壶
teapot

糖盒
sugar bowl

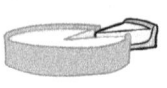
一份饭菜
portion

意式咖啡机
espresso machine

高脚椅
high chair

账单
bill

托盘
tray

刀
knife

餐叉
fork

勺子
spoon

茶匙
teaspoon

餐巾
serviette

玻璃杯
glass

餐馆 - restaurant

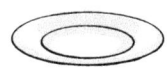
碟子
plate

汤盘
soup plate

碟子
saucer

酱
sauce

盐瓶
salt shaker

胡椒磨
pepper mill

醋
vinegar

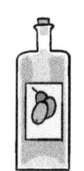
食用油
oil

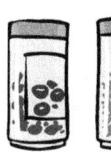
调味料
spices

番茄酱
ketchup

芥末
mustard

蛋黄酱
mayonnaise

餐馆 - restaurant

超市
supermarket

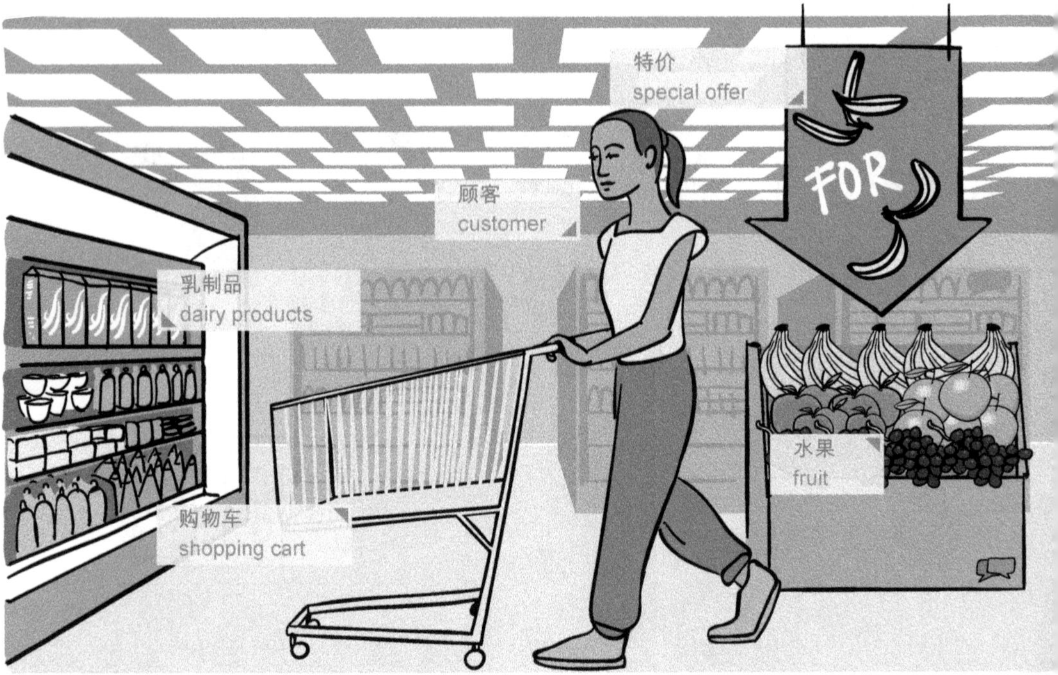

特价
special offer
FOR
顾客
customer
乳制品
dairy products
水果
fruit
购物车
shopping cart

BUTCHERS

肉铺

butcher's shop

BAKERY

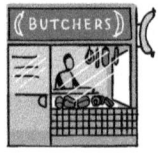

面包房

bakery

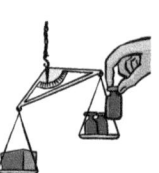

称重

weigh

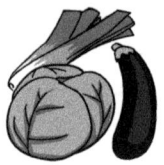

蔬菜

vegetables

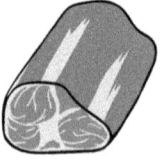

肉

meat

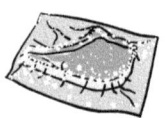

冷冻食品

frozen food

冷盘
cold cuts

罐头食品
canned food

洗衣粉
detergent

甜食
candy

日用品
household products

清洁用品
cleaning products

销售员
sales representative

收银机
cash register

收银员
cashier

购物清单
shopping list

开放时间
opening hours

钱包
wallet

信用卡
credit card

袋子
bag

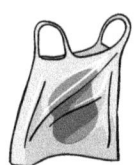
塑料袋
plastic bag

超市 - supermarket

饮料
drinks

水
water

果汁
juice

牛奶
milk

可乐
coke

红酒
wine

啤酒
beer

酒
alcohol

可可
cocoa

茶
tea

咖啡
coffee

意式浓缩咖啡
espresso

卡布奇诺
cappuccino

食物
food

香蕉
banana

苹果
apple

橙子
orange

西瓜
melon

柠檬
lemon

胡萝卜
carrot

大蒜
garlic

竹子
bamboo

洋葱
onion

蘑菇
mushroom

坚果
nuts

面条
noodles

意大利面条
spaghetti

米饭
rice

沙拉
salad

薯条
fries

炸土豆
fried potatoes

披萨饼
pizza

汉堡包
hamburger

三明治
sandwich

炸猪排
escalope

火腿
ham

萨拉米
salami

香肠
sausage

鸡肉
chicken

烤肉
roast

鱼
fish

燕麦片
porridge oats

穆兹利
muesli

玉米片
cornflakes

面粉
flour

羊角面包
croissant

面包卷
bread roll

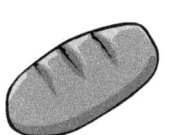
面包
bread

烤面包
toast

饼干
cookies

黄油
butter

凝乳
curd

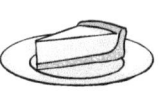
蛋糕
cake

蛋
egg

煎蛋
fried egg

奶酪
cheese

食物 - food

25

冰激凌
ice cream

糖
sugar

蜂蜜
honey

果酱
jelly

巧克力酱
nougat cream

咖喱饭
curry

食物 - food

农场
farm

农舍 farm house
粮仓 barn
稻草捆 straw bale
田野 field
马 horse
拖车 trailer
拖拉机 tractor
马驹 foal
驴 donkey
羔羊 lamb
羊 sheep

山羊
goat

奶牛
cow

牛犊
calf

猪
pig

小猪
piglet

公牛
bull

农场 - farm

鹅
goose

鸭
duck

小鸡
chick

母鸡
hen

公鸡
cockerel

鼠
rat

猫
cat

老鼠
mouse

牛
ox

狗
dog

狗屋
dog house

花园浇水软管
garden hose

洒水壶
watering can

长柄大镰刀
scythe

犁
plough

农场 - farm

镰刀
sickle

锄头
hoe

长柄草耙
pitchfork

斧头
axe

独轮手推车
pushcart

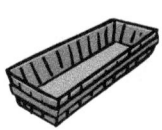
饲料槽
trough

牛奶罐
milk can

麻布袋
sack

栅栏
fence

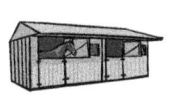
马厩
stable

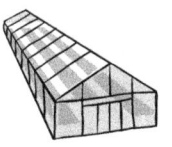
温室
greenhouse

土壤
soil

种子
seed

肥料
fertilizer

联合收割机
combine harvester

收割
harvest

收割
harvest

山药
yams

小麦
wheat

大豆
soya

土豆
potato

玉米
corn

油菜籽
rapeseed

果树
fruit tree

树薯
manioc

谷物
grain

房子
house

烟囱 chimney
屋顶 roof
落水管 downspout
窗户 window
车库 garage
门铃 doorbell
门 door
垃圾桶 trash can
信箱 mailbox
花园 garden

客厅
living room

浴室
bathroom

厨房
kitchen

卧室
bedroom

儿童房
child's room

餐厅
dining room

房子 - house

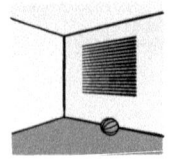
地板
floor

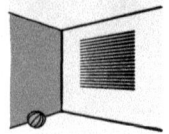
墙壁
wall

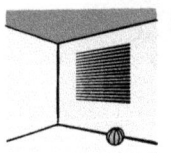
吊顶
ceiling

地窖
cellar

桑拿
sauna

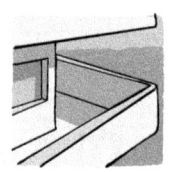
阳台
balcony

露台
terrace

游泳池
pool

割草机
lawn mower

被单
sheet

床罩
bedspread

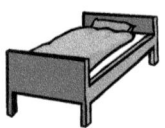
床
bed

扫帚
broom

水桶
bucket

开关
switch

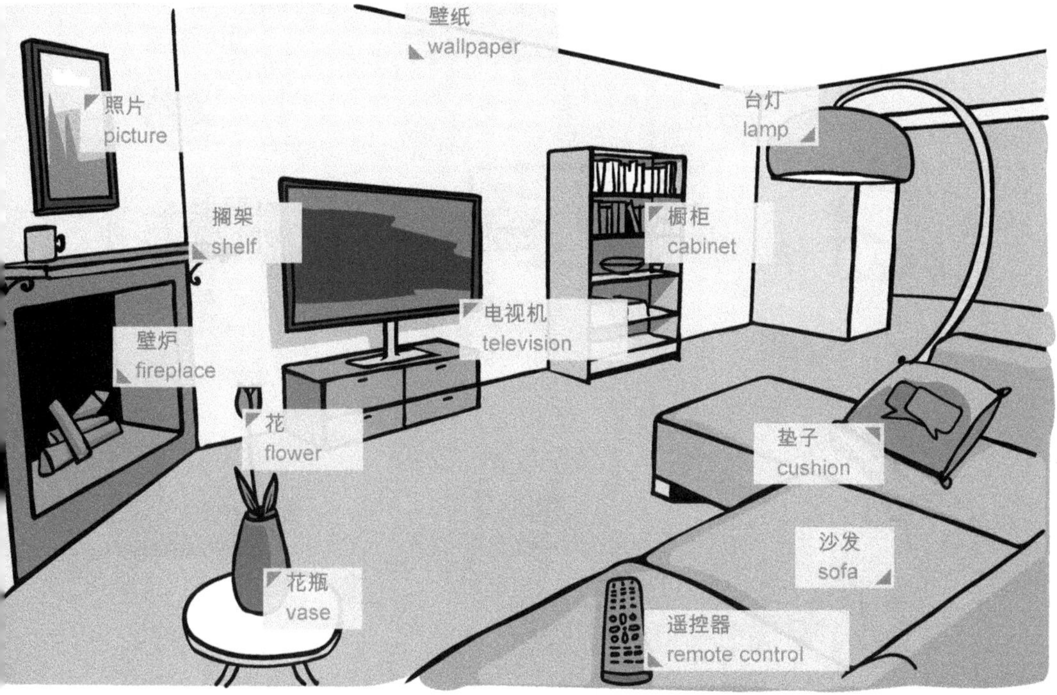

客厅
living room

- 壁纸 wallpaper
- 照片 picture
- 台灯 lamp
- 搁架 shelf
- 橱柜 cabinet
- 壁炉 fireplace
- 电视机 television
- 花 flower
- 垫子 cushion
- 花瓶 vase
- 沙发 sofa
- 遥控器 remote control

地毯
carpet

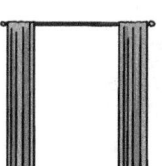

窗帘
drape

餐桌
table

椅子
chair

摇椅
rocking chair

扶手椅
armchair

 书 book	 毯子 blanket	 装饰品 decoration
 木柴 firewood	 电影 film	 高保真音响 stereo system
 钥匙 key	 报纸 newspaper	 油画 painting
 海报 poster	 收音机 radio	 笔记本 notebook
 吸尘器 vacuum cleaner	 仙人掌 cactus	 蜡烛 candle

客厅 - living room

厨房
kitchen

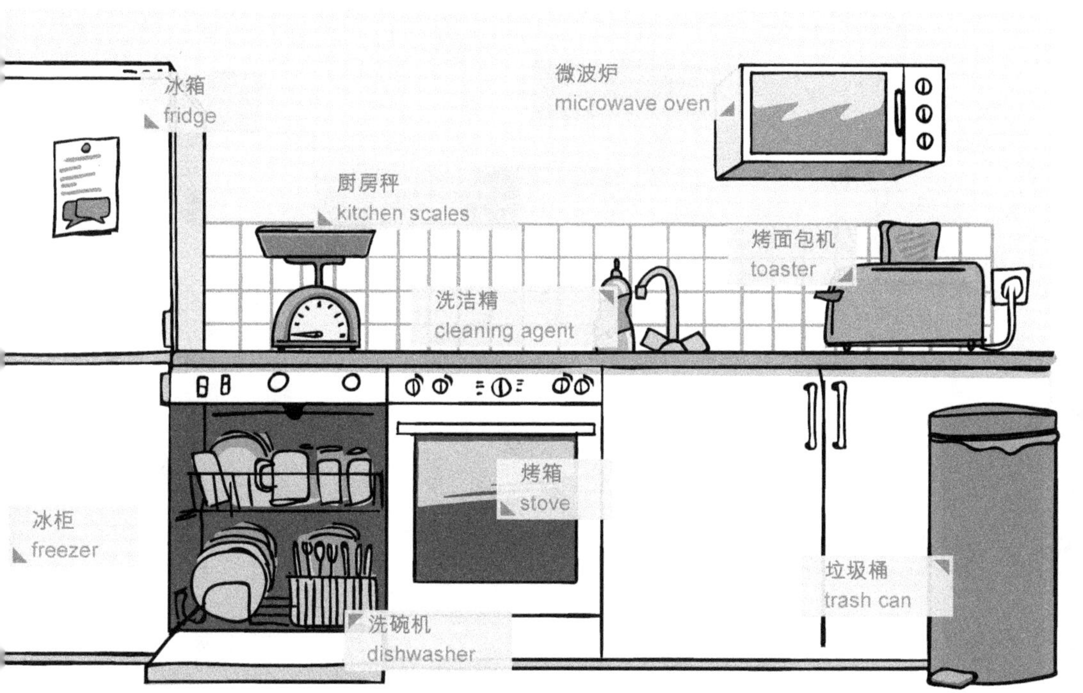

冰箱 / fridge
微波炉 / microwave oven
厨房秤 / kitchen scales
烤面包机 / toaster
洗洁精 / cleaning agent
冰柜 / freezer
烤箱 / stove
垃圾桶 / trash can
洗碗机 / dishwasher

炊具
cooker

锅
pot

铸铁锅
cast-iron pot

炒锅
wok / kadai

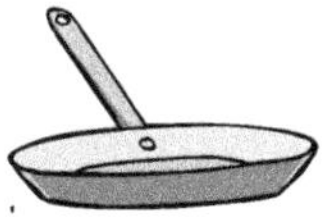

平底锅
pan

水壶
kettle

厨房 - kitchen

蒸锅
steamer

烤盘
baking tray

陶瓷锅
crockery

马克杯
mug

碗
bowl

筷子
chopsticks

长柄勺
ladle

铲子
spatula

搅拌器
whisk

滤网
strainer

筛子
sieve

磨碎机
grater

研钵
mortar

烧烤
barbecue

明火
fireplace

厨房 - kitchen

菜板
chopping board

擀面杖
rolling pin

开瓶器
corkscrew

罐子
can

开罐器
can opener

隔热手套
oven cloth

水槽
sink

刷子
brush

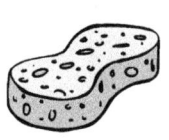
海绵
sponge

搅拌机
blender

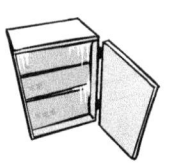
冷藏箱
deep freezer

奶瓶
baby bottle

水龙头
tap

厨房 - kitchen

浴室
bathroom

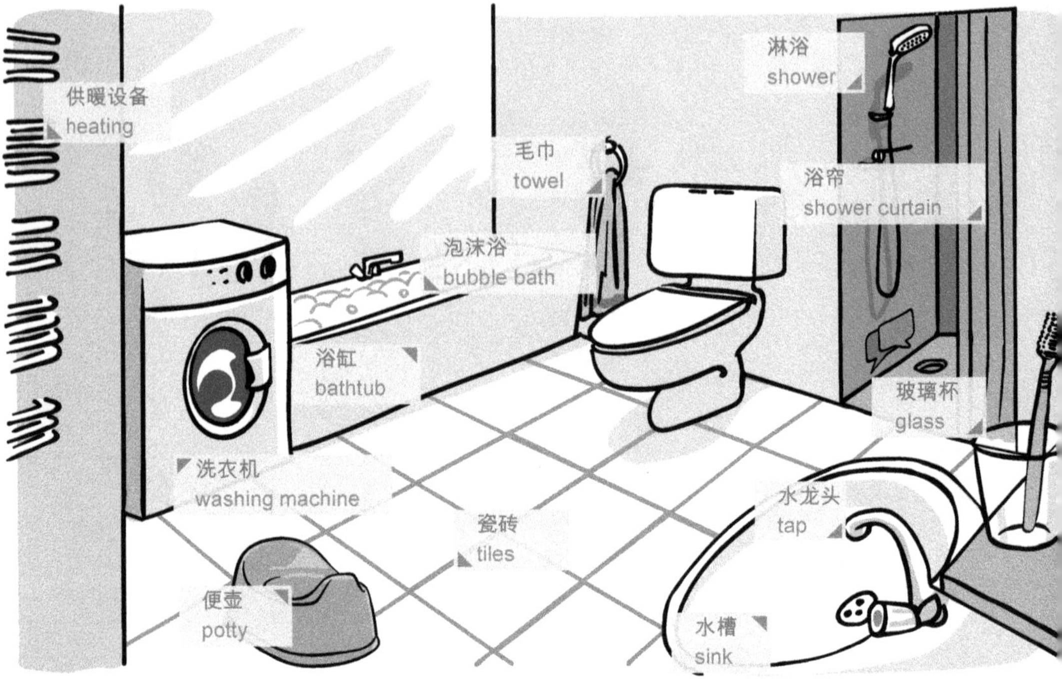

- 供暖设备 heating
- 淋浴 shower
- 毛巾 towel
- 浴帘 shower curtain
- 泡沫浴 bubble bath
- 浴缸 bathtub
- 玻璃杯 glass
- 洗衣机 washing machine
- 瓷砖 tiles
- 水龙头 tap
- 便壶 potty
- 水槽 sink

厕所 toilet	蹲便器 squat toilet	坐浴器 bidet
小便池 urinal	厕纸 toilet paper	马桶刷 toilet brush

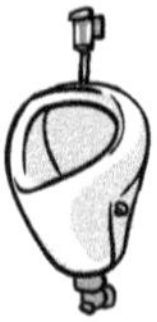

浴室 - bathroom

牙刷
toothbrush

牙膏
toothpaste

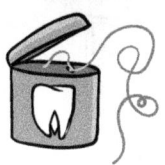
牙线
dental floss

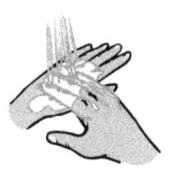
洗
wash

手持式喷淋头
hand shower

冲洗器
douche

洗脸盆
basin

擦背刷
back brush

肥皂
soap

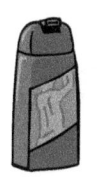
沐浴露
shower gel

洗发水
shampoo

法兰绒
flannel

排水
drain

乳霜
creme

除臭剂
deodorant

浴室 - bathroom

镜子
mirror

手镜
hand mirror

剃须刀
razor

剃须泡沫
shaving foam

须后水
aftershave

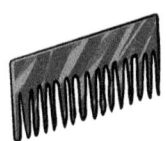
梳子
comb

刷子
brush

吹风机
hair-dryer

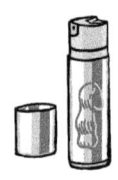
喷发定型剂
hairspray

化妆品
makeup

唇膏
lipstick

指甲油
nail varnish

化妆棉
cotton wool

指甲剪
nail scissors

香水
perfume

浴室 - bathroom

洗漱包
washbag

凳子
stool

计重秤
weighing scales

浴袍
bathrobe

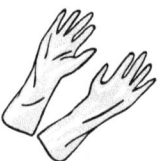
橡胶手套
rubber gloves

卫生棉条
tampon

卫生巾
sanitary towel

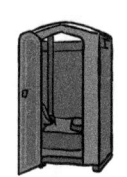
化学厕所
chemical toilet

浴室 - bathroom

儿童房

child's room

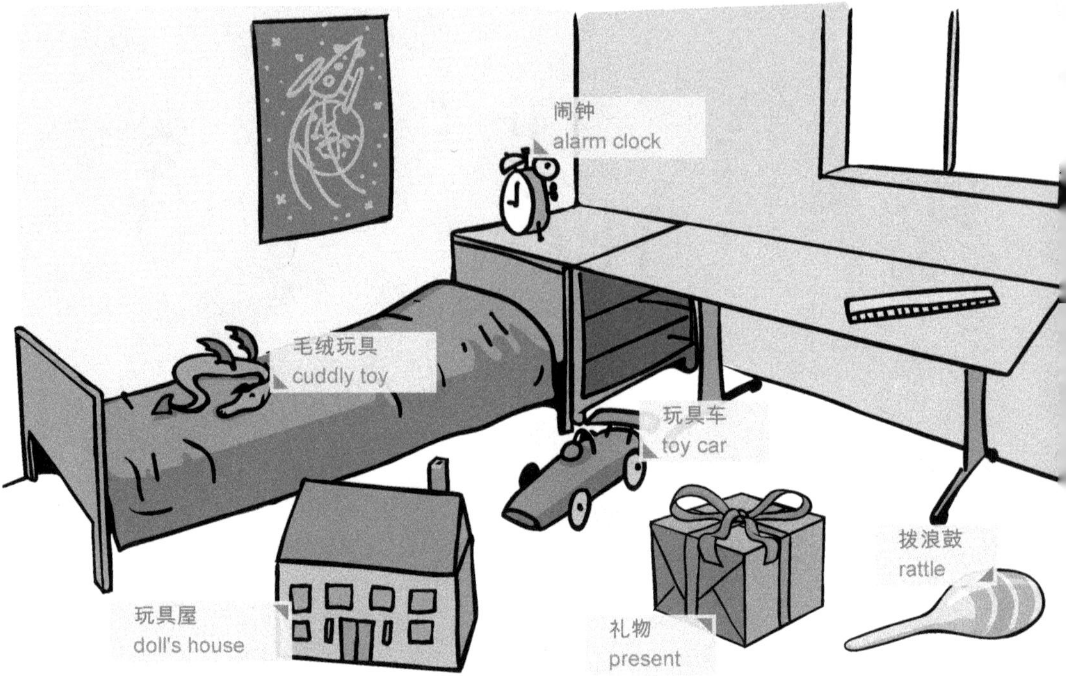
闹钟
alarm clock
毛绒玩具
cuddly toy
玩具车
toy car
拨浪鼓
rattle
玩具屋
doll's house
礼物
present

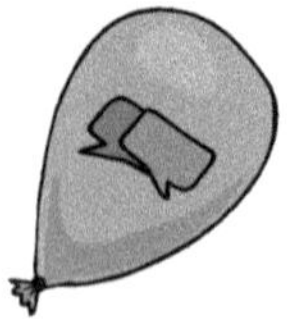

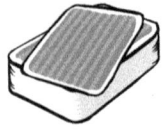

气球

balloon

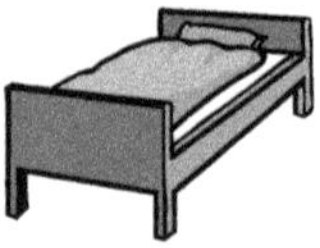

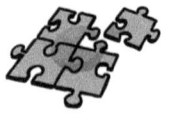

床

bed

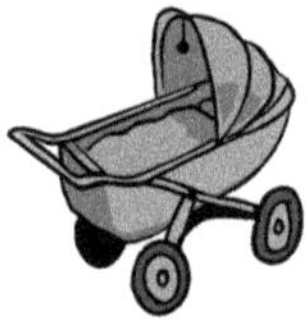

（洋娃娃用）婴儿车

stroller

扑克牌

deck of cards

拼图

jigsaw

SUPER MEGA

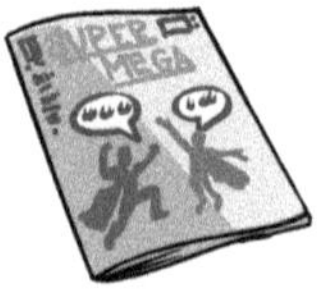

漫画

comic

乐高积木
lego bricks

积木玩具
toy blocks

玩具人
action figure

婴儿服
romper suit

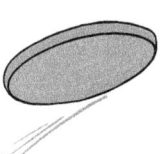
飞盘
frisbee

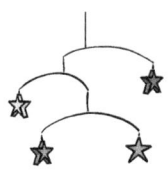
床铃玩具
mobile

棋盘游戏
board game

骰子
dice

火车模型
model train set

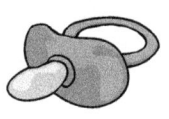
安抚奶嘴
dummy

聚会
party

绘本
picture book

球
ball

洋娃娃
doll

玩
play

儿童房 - child's room

沙坑
sandpit

秋千
swing

玩具
toy

游戏机
video game console

三轮车
tricycle

泰迪熊
teddy bear

衣柜
wardrobe

衣服
clothing

袜子
socks

长袜
stockings

紧身裤
tights

身体
body

裤子
pants

牛仔裤
jeans

短裙
skirt

女式衬衫
blouse

衬衫
shirt

套头衫
pullover

卫衣
sweater

西装夹克
blazer

夹克
jacket

外套
coat

雨衣
raincoat

套装
costume

连衣裙
dress

婚纱
wedding dress

西装
suit

睡袍
nightgown

睡衣
pajamas

莎丽
sari

头巾
headscarf

包头巾
turban

波卡
burka

卡夫坦
kaftan

(阿拉伯式)长袍
abaya

泳衣
swimsuit

男式泳裤
trunks

短裤
shorts

运动服
tracksuit

围裙
apron

手套
gloves

衣服 - clothing

纽扣
button

眼镜
glasses

手链
bracelet

项链
necklace

戒指
ring

耳环
earring

便帽
cap

衣架
coat hanger

帽子
hat

领带
tie

拉链
zip

头盔
helmet

背带
braces

校服
school uniform

制服
uniform

围兜
bib

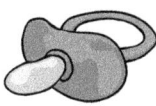
安抚奶嘴
dummy

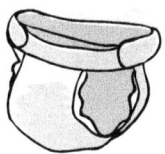
尿不湿
diaper

办公室
office

- 服务器 server
- 文件柜 filing cabinet
- 打印机 printer
- 显示屏 monitor
- 纸 paper
- 办公桌 desk
- 鼠标 mouse
- 文件夹 folder
- 键盘 keyboard
- 废纸筐 waste-paper basket
- 电脑 computer
- 椅子 chair

咖啡杯
coffee mug

计算器
calculator

因特网
internet

办公室 - office

笔记本电脑
laptop

信件
letter

消息
message

手机
cell phone

网络
network

复印机
photocopier

软件
software

电话
telephone

插座
plug socket

传真机
fax machine

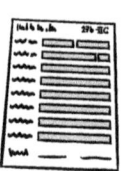
表格
form

文件
document

办公室 - office

经济
economy

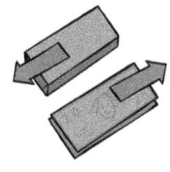
买
buy

付钱
pay

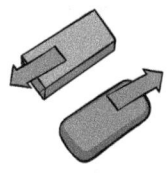
交易
trade

现金
money

美元
dollar

欧元
euro

日元
yen

卢布
rouble

瑞士法郎
Swiss franc

人民币
renminbi yuan

卢比
rupee

提款处
cash point

外币兑换处
currency exchange office

金
gold

银
silver

石油
oil

能源
energy

价格
price

合同
contract

税金
tax

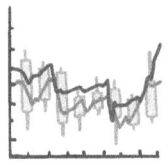
股票
stock

工作
work

职员
employee

老板
employer

工厂
factory

商店
shop

经济 - economy

职业
occupations

警官 / police officer

消防员 / fireman

厨师 / cook

医生 / doctor

飞行员 / pilot

园丁
gardener

木匠
carpenter

裁缝
seamstress

法官
judge

化学家
chemist

演员
actor

职业 - occupations

公交车司机
bus driver

出租车司机
taxi driver

渔夫
fisherman

清洁女工
cleaning lady

屋顶工
roofer

服务员
waiter

猎人
hunter

画家
painter

面包师
baker

电工
electrician

建筑工人
builder

工程师
engineer

屠夫
butcher

水管工
plumber

邮递员
postman

职业 - occupations

士兵
soldier

建筑师
architect

收银员
cashier

花农
florist

理发师
hairdresser

售票员
conductor

机械师
mechanic

船长
captain

牙医
dentist

科学家
scientist

拉比
rabbi

伊玛目
imam

和尚
monk

牧师
pastor

工具
tools

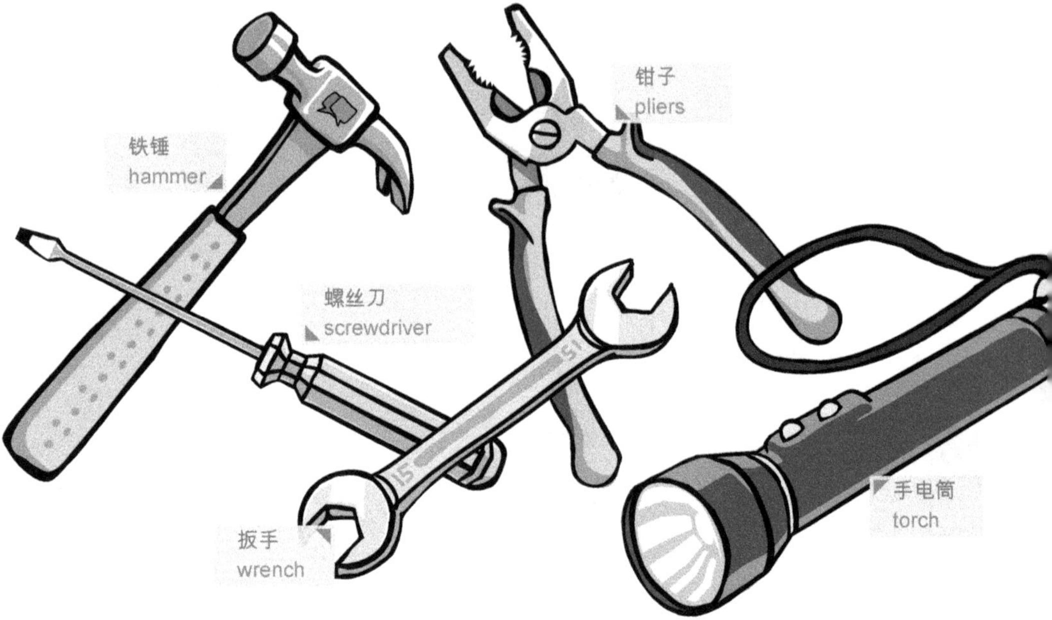

铁锤 hammer

钳子 pliers

螺丝刀 screwdriver

扳手 wrench

手电筒 torch

挖掘机
excavator

工具箱
toolbox

梯子
ladder

锯子
saw

钉子
nails

钻机
drill

修
repair

铲子
shovel

靠!
Damn!

簸箕
dustpan

油漆桶
paint can

螺丝
screws

乐器
musical instruments

低音提琴
double bass

打击乐器
drum set

扬声器
loud speaker

小号
trumpet

吉他
guitar

钢琴
piano

小提琴
violin

贝斯
bass

定音鼓
timpani

鼓
drums

电子琴
keyboard

萨克斯管
saxophone

长笛
flute

麦克风
microphone

乐器 - musical instruments

动物园
ZOO

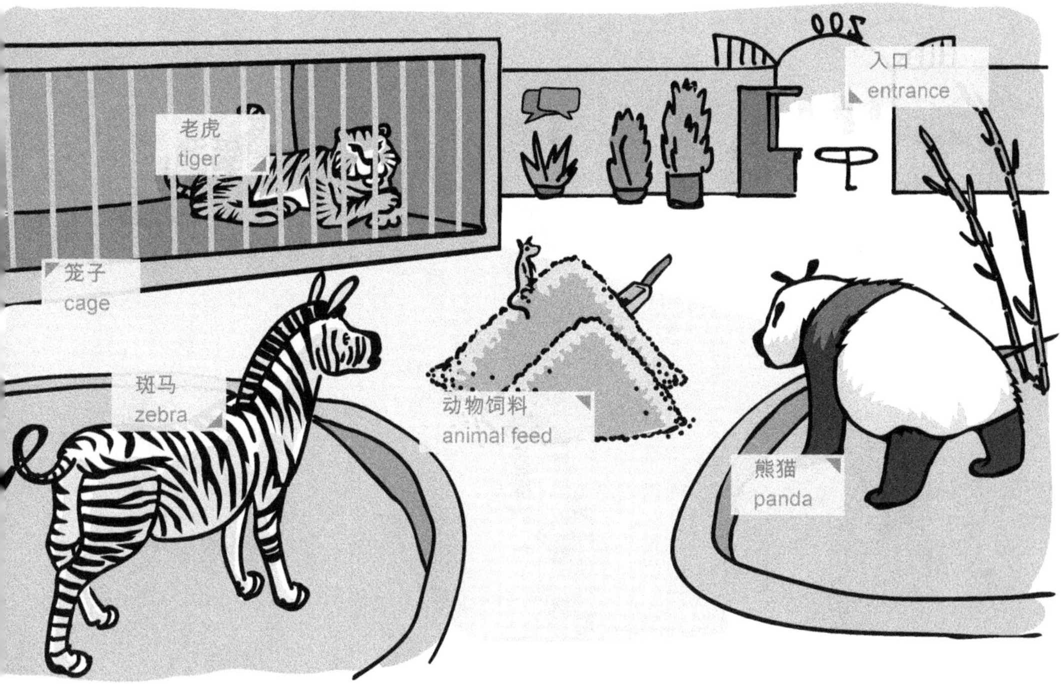

- 老虎 tiger
- 入口 entrance
- 笼子 cage
- 斑马 zebra
- 动物饲料 animal feed
- 熊猫 panda

动物
animals

大象
elephant

袋鼠
kangaroo

犀牛
rhino

大猩猩
gorilla

熊
bear

动物园 - zoo

骆驼
camel

鸵鸟
ostrich

狮子
lion

猴子
monkey

火烈鸟
flamingo

鹦鹉
parrot

北极熊
polar bear

企鹅
penguin

鲨鱼
shark

孔雀
peacock

蛇
snake

鳄鱼
crocodile

动物园管理员
zookeeper

海豹
seal

美洲豹
jaguar

动物园 - ZOO

矮种马

pony

豹

leopard

河马

hippo

长颈鹿

giraffe

老鹰

eagle

野猪

boar

鱼

fish

龟

turtle

海象

walrus

狐狸

fox

羚羊

gazelle

动物园 - zoo

体育
sports

活动
activities

活动 - activities

 有 have	 做 do	 当 be
 站 stand	 跑 run	 拉 pull
 扔 throw	 摔倒 fall	 躺 lie
 等待 wait	 携带 carry	 坐 sit
 穿衣 get dressed	 睡觉 sleep	 醒来 wake up

活动 - activities

看
look at

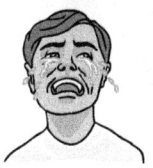
哭
cry

抚摸
stroke

梳头
comb

交谈
talk

明白
understand

问
ask

听
listen

喝
drink

吃
eat

清理
tidy up

爱
love

做饭
cook

开车
drive

飞
fly

活动 - activities

航行
sail

计算
calculate

读
read

学习
learn

工作
work

结婚
marry

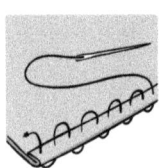
缝
sew

刷牙
brush teeth

杀
kill

抽烟
smoke

寄
send

活动 - activities

家
family

- 祖母 grandmother
- 祖父 grandfather
- 父亲 father
- 母亲 mother
- 婴童 baby
- 女儿 daughter
- 儿子 son

客人
guest

阿姨
aunt

叔叔
uncle

兄弟
brother

姐妹
sister

家 - family

身体
body

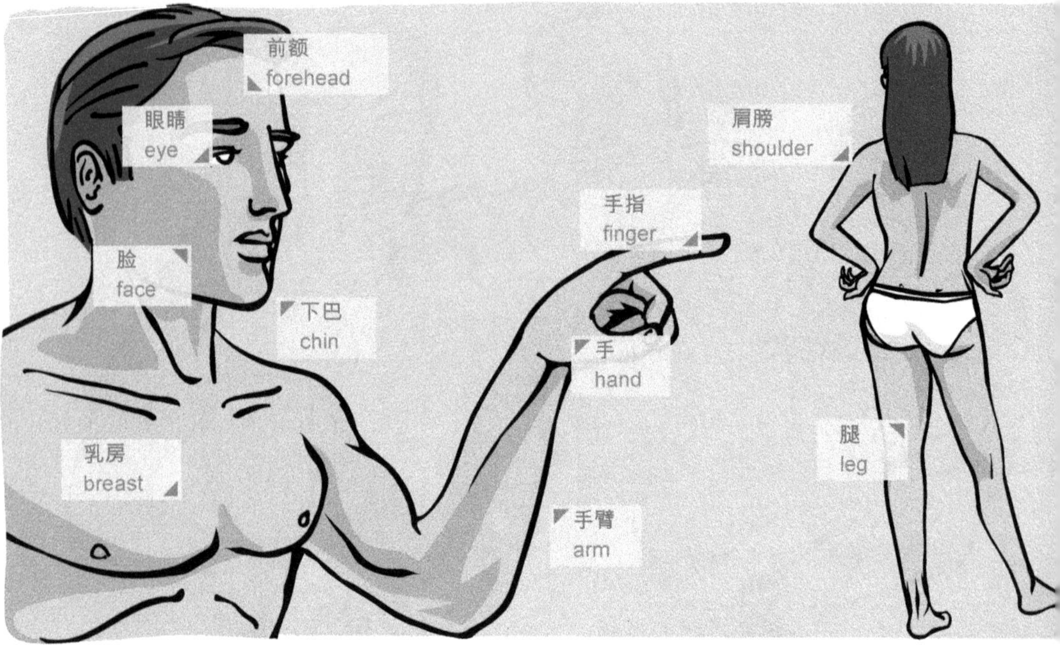

- 前额 forehead
- 眼睛 eye
- 脸 face
- 下巴 chin
- 乳房 breast
- 肩膀 shoulder
- 手指 finger
- 手 hand
- 手臂 arm
- 腿 leg

婴童
baby

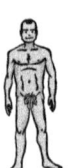

男人
man

女人
woman

女孩
girl

男孩
boy

头
head

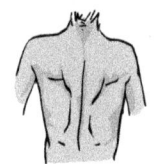
背部
back

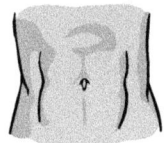
肚子
belly

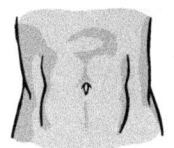
肚脐
navel

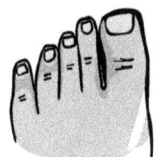
脚趾
toe

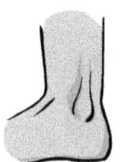
脚后跟
heel

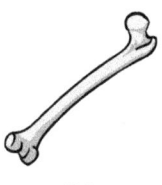
骨头
bone

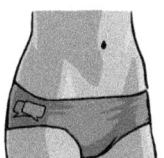
臀部
hip

膝盖
knee

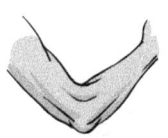
手肘
elbow

鼻子
nose

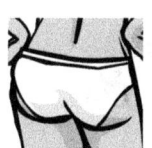
屁股
buttocks

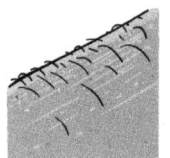
皮肤
skin

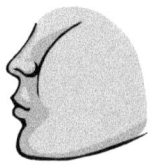
脸颊
cheek

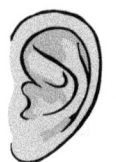
耳朵
ear

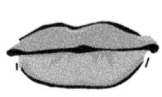
嘴唇
lip

身体 - body

69

嘴
mouth

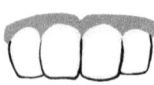
牙齿
tooth

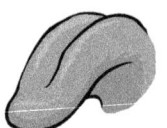
舌头
tongue

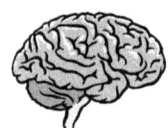
脑
brain

心脏
heart

肌肉
muscle

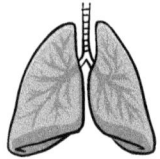
肺
lung

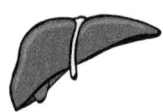
肝脏
liver

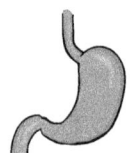
胃
stomach

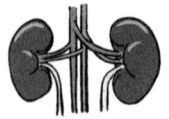
肾脏
kidneys

性交
sex

避孕套
condom

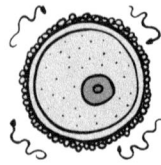
卵子
ovum

精子
semen

怀孕
pregnancy

身体 - body

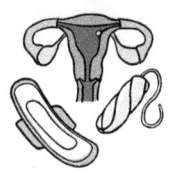
月经
menstruation

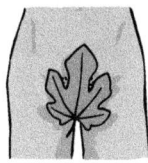
阴道
vagina

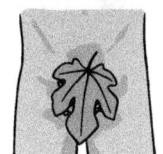
阴茎
penis

眉毛
eyebrow

头发
hair

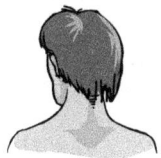
脖子
neck

身体 - body

医院
hospital

医院 hospital
救护车 ambulance
轮椅 wheelchair
骨折 fracture

医生
doctor

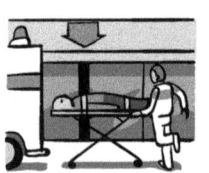

急诊室
emergency room

护士
nurse

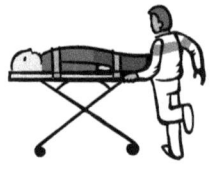

紧急情况
emergency

昏迷
unconscious

痛
pain

医院 - hospital

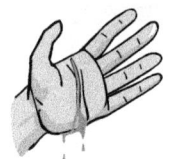 受伤 injury	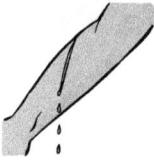 出血 bleeding	 心脏病发作 heart attack
 中风 stroke	 过敏 allergy	 咳嗽 cough
 发烧 fever	 流感 flu	 腹泻 diarrhea
 头痛 headache	 癌症 cancer	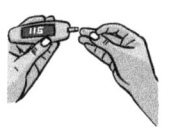 糖尿病 diabetes
 外科医生 surgeon	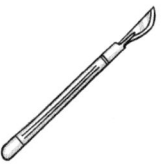 手术刀 scalpel	 手术 operation

医院 - hospital

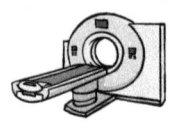	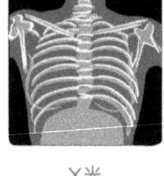	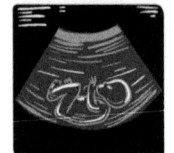
CT CT	X光 x-ray	超声波 ultrasound

口罩 face mask	疾病 disease	候诊室 waiting room
	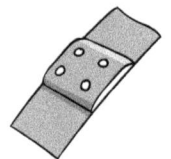	
拐杖 crutch	石膏 plaster	绷带 bandage
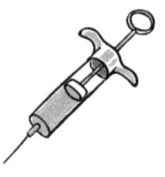	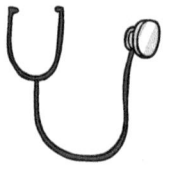	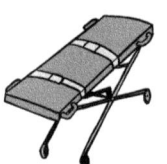
注射 injection	听诊器 stethoscope	担架 stretcher

体温计 clinical thermometer	出生 birth	超重 overweight

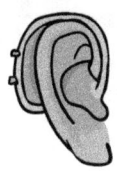
助听器
hearing aid

消毒液
disinfectant

感染
infection

病毒
virus

艾滋病
HIV / AIDS

药物
medicine

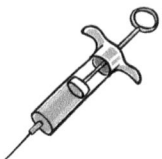
接种疫苗
vaccination

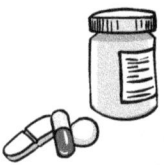
药片
tablets

药丸
pill

急救电话
emergency call

血压计
blood pressure monitor

生病/健康
ill / healthy

医院 - hospital

紧急情况
emergency

救命！
Help!

警报
alarm

突击
assault

攻击
attack

危险
danger

紧急出口
emergency exit

着火啦！
Fire!

灭火器
fire extinguisher

意外
accident

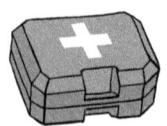
急救箱
first-aid kit

呼救信号
SOS

警察
police

地球
earth

欧洲
Europe

北美洲
North America

南美洲
South America

非洲
Africa

亚洲
Asia

澳洲
Australia

大西洋
Atlantic

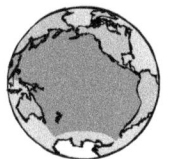
太平洋
Pacific

印度洋
Indian Ocean

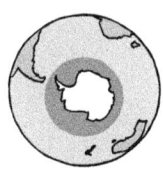
南冰洋
Antarctic Ocean

北冰洋
Arctic Ocean

北极
North pole

南极
South pole

南极洲
Antarctica

地球
earth

陆地
land

海
sea

岛
island

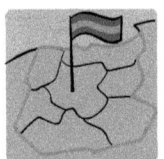
国家
nation

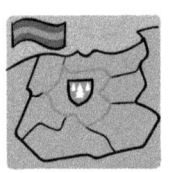
国家
state

钟表
clock

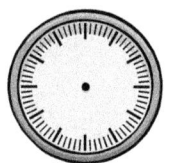
钟面
clock face

时针
hour hand

分针
minute hand

秒针
second hand

现在几点？
What time is it?

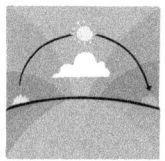
天
day

时间
time

现在
now

电子表
digital watch

分
minute

时
hour

周
week

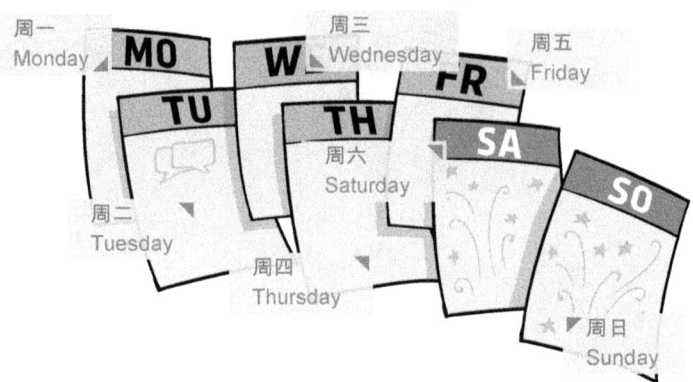

周一 Monday
周二 Tuesday
周三 Wednesday
周四 Thursday
周五 Friday
周六 Saturday
周日 Sunday

昨天
yesterday

今天
today

明天
tomorrow

早晨
morning

中午
noon

晚上
evening

工作日
workdays

周末
weekend

年

year

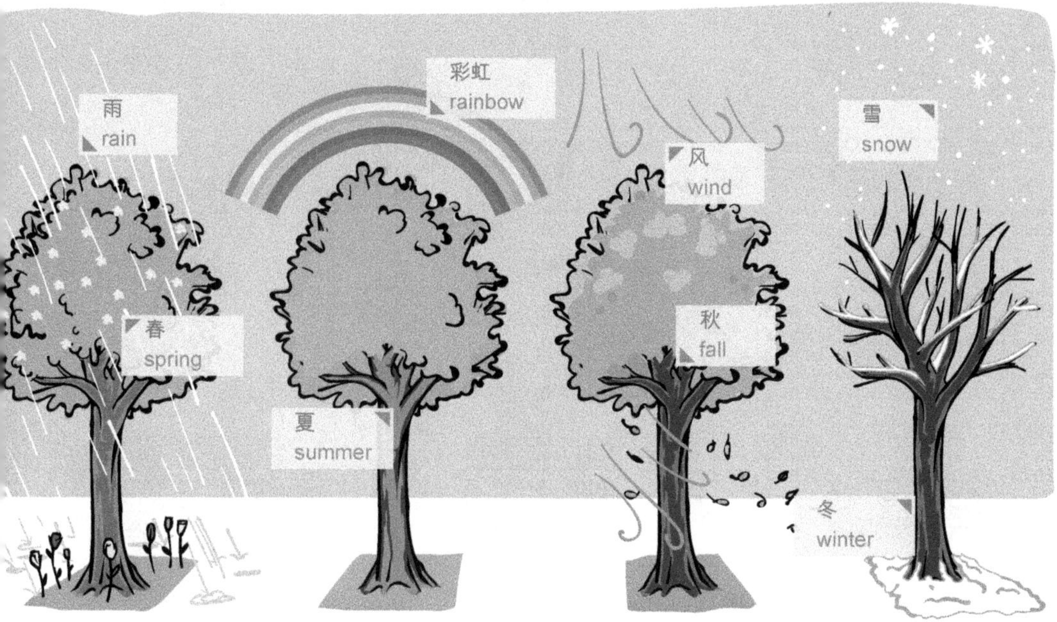

雨
rain
彩虹
rainbow
风
wind
雪
snow
春
spring
夏
summer
秋
fall
冬
winter

4.APRIL 11°
5.APRIL 4°
6.APRIL 13°
7.APRIL 8°
8.APRIL 10°

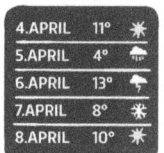

天气预报

weather forecast

F
120
90
60
30
0
-30
C
40
30
20
10
0
-10
-20

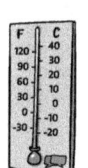

温度计

thermometer

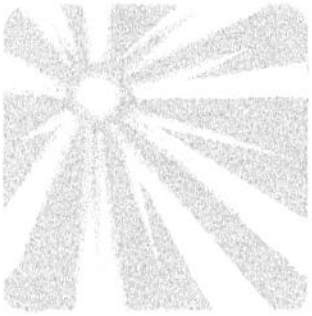

阳光

sunshine

云

cloud

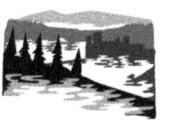

雾

fog

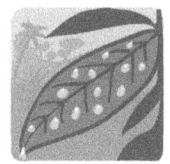

潮湿

humidity

闪电
lightning

打雷
thunder

风暴
storm

冰雹
hail

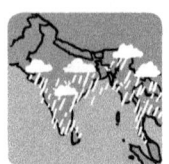
季风
monsoon

洪水
flood

冰
ice

一月
January

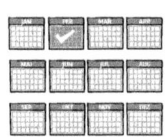
二月
February

三月
March

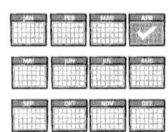
四月
April

五月
May

六月
June

七月
July

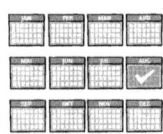
八月
August

年 - year

九月
September

十月
October

十一月
November

十二月
December

形状
shapes

圆形
circle

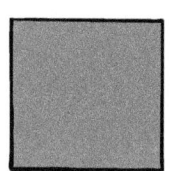
正方形
square

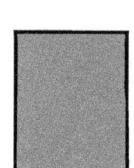
长方形
rectangle

三角形
triangle

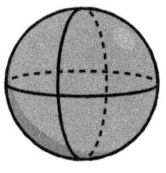
球体
sphere

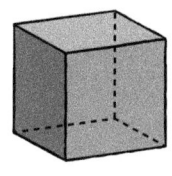
立方体
cube

颜色
colors

白
white

黄
yellow

橙
orange

粉
pink

红
red

紫
purple

蓝
blue

绿
green

棕
brown

灰
gray

黑
black

反义词
opposites

很多/少许
a lot / a little

生气/平静
angry / calm

美/丑
beautiful / ugly

首/尾
beginning / end

大/小
big / small

明/暗
bright / dark

兄弟/姐妹
brother / sister

干净/肮脏
clean / dirty

完整/缺失
complete / incomplete

白天/晚上
day / night

死/生
dead / alive

宽/窄
wide / narrow

反义词 - opposites

可食用/非食用
edible / inedible

邪恶/善良
evil / kind

兴奋/无聊
excited / bored

胖/瘦
fat / thin

第一/最后
first / last

朋友/敌人
friend / enemy

满/空
full / empty

硬/软
hard / soft

重/轻
heavy / light

饿/渴
hunger / thirst

生病/健康
ill / healthy

非法/合法
illegal / legal

聪明/愚笨
intelligent / stupid

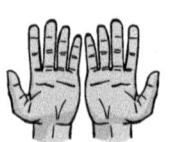
左/右
left / right

近/远
near / far

反义词 - opposites

新/旧
new / used

没有/有些
nothing / something

老/幼
old / young

开/关
on / off

打开/合上
open / closed

安静/吵闹
quiet / loud

富/穷
rich / poor

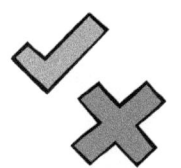

对/错
right / wrong

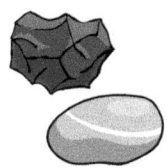

粗糙/光滑
rough / smooth

伤心/高兴
sad / happy

短/长
short / long

慢/快
slow / fast

湿/干
wet / dry

温暖/凉爽
warm / cool

战争/和平
war / peace

反义词 - opposites

数字
numbers

0 零 zero

1 一 one

2 二 two

3 三 three

4 四 four

5 五 five

6 六 six

7 七 seven

8 八 eight

9 九 nine

10 十 ten

11 十一 eleven

12
十二
twelve

13
十三
thirteen

14
十四
fourteen

15
十五
fifteen

16
十六
sixteen

17
十七
seventeen

18
十八
eighteen

19
十九
nineteen

20
二十
twenty

100
百
hundred

1.000
千
thousand

1.000.000
百万
million

数字 - numbers

语言
languages

英语
English

美式英语
American English

普通话
Chinese Mandarin

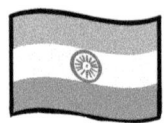

印地语
Hindi

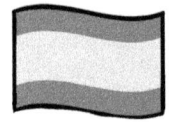

西班牙语
Spanish

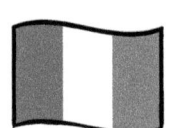

法语
French

阿拉伯语
Arabic

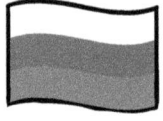

俄语
Russian

葡萄牙语
Portuguese

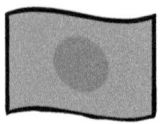

孟加拉语
Bengali

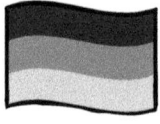

德语
German

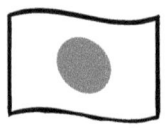

日语
Japanese

谁/什么/怎样
who / what / how

我
I

你
you

他/她/它
he / she / it

我们
we

你们
you

他们
they

谁？
who?

什么？
what?

怎样？
how?

哪里？
where?

什么时候？
when?

名字
name

方位
where

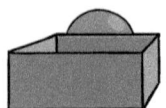
后面
behind

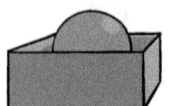
里面
in

前面
in front of

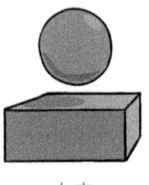
上方
over

上面
on

下面
under

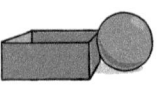
旁边
beside

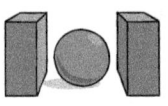
中间
between

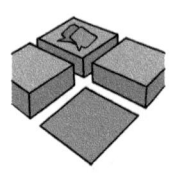
地点
place

CPSIA information can be obtained
at www.ICGtesting.com
Printed in the USA
LVHW050420300920
667478LV00005B/723